RICHARD LICHFIELD

The Trimming of
Thomas Nash
1597

The Scolar Press
1973

ISBN 0 85417 917 8

Printed in Great Britain by
The Scolar Press Limited
Menston, Yorkshire, England

NOTE

Reproduced (original size) from a copy in the Bodleian Library, by permission of the Curators. Shelf-mark: Arch A f 78.

The Trimming of Thomas Nashe was the last publication to arise from the controversy between Gabriel Harvey and Thomas Nash. The quarrel had started eight years earlier with the appearance of the anonymous poem *Pap with a hatchet* in 1589, but the roots of the differences between the two sides lay in the Martin Marprelate controversy. After *Pap with a hatchet*, Gabriel Harvey's brother Richard published *Plain Perceval*, and this was followed by Robert Greene's *Menaphon* containing a preface by Thomas Nash.

At this stage direct accusations and personal abuse had not yet begun, but in 1590 Richard Harvey published *Lamb of God* which specifically attacked Nash for his preface to *Menaphon*. Even so, it seems as though the quarrel could have ended there, because it was a further two years before Greene published his *Quip for an upstart courtier* and attacked all three Harvey brothers.

After this Harvey and Nash set to in earnest and accusations and counter-accusations followed each other from alternate sides with scarcely a pause between them. The precise order in which some of the publications appeared is not certain, but in all probability it was as follows:

Nash *Pierce Penniless*, 1592
Harvey *Four letters*, 1592
Nash *Strange news* 1593
Harvey *Pierce's supererogation* 1593
Nash *Christ's tears over Jerusalem* 1593
Harvey *A new letter* 1593
Nash *Christ's tears* (second ed.) 1594
Nash *Have with you to Saffron Walden* 1596

Doubt has been expressed about the authorship of *Trimming* although the usual conjecture is that it was written by Harvey. In his edition of Nash's *Works* (5 vols., 1908-10, reprinted 1958 ed. F. P. Wilson), R. B. McKerrow pointed out that the style of *Trimming* is quite different from Harvey's, Harvey is never defended or justified and is referred to only once, and *Trimming* is a reply to the dedication only of Nash's *Have with you to Saffron Walden*. Nevertheless, McKerrow assumed Harvey to be the author since there was no definite proof that he was not.

Have with you to Saffron Walden is dedicated to the barber of Trinity College, Cambridge, 'Don Richardo Barbarossa de Caesario', and the information printed in *Trimming* (on the title-page and at the end of the preface) states quite clearly that *Trimming* was written by this same barber, Richard Lichfield. In view of this and the other internal evidence mentioned by McKerrow, there seems to be no reason why Richard Lichfield should not be accepted as the author.

Trimming was entered in the *Stationers' Register* to Cuthbert Burby on 11th October 1597, but further uncertainty surrounds the name 'Philip Scarlet' printed on the title-page. The work may have been transferred from Burby to Scarlet, but nothing is known of Scarlet and *Trimming* seems to have been the only book with which he was involved. There was a Cambridge book-seller called Philip Scarlet who was operating from 1605 to 1634 but there is no other evidence to link him with *Trimming*, and it is possible that the Philip Scarlet mentioned on the title-page was a pseudonym.

Nash planned to reply to *Trimming* and in *Lenten stuff*, 1599, he remarks that he has 'a pamphlet hot a brooding that shall be called the *Barbers warming panne*' (pp. 1-2). Furthermore, it appears that Nash did not regard Harvey as the author of *Trimming* since the *Barbers warming panne* was to be directed against 'the silliest millers thombe, or contemptible stickle-banck of [his] enemies', and in the ranks of Nash's enemies Harvey surely could not be dismissed in such terms.

It seems likely that *Barbers warming panne* never appeared because of the ban which the Stationers' Company put on all works by Nash and Harvey, resolving:

> That all Nasshes bookes and Doctor Harvyes bookes be taken wheresoever they maye be found and that none of theire bookes bee ever printed hereafter.
> (E. Arber *A transcript of the Registers of the Company of Stationers*, 1875-77, Vol. III p. 667.)

Trimming was reprinted in Harvey's *Works*, edited by A. B. Grosart, Vol. III, 1884-85, pp. 3-72.

Reference: STC. 12906.

THE
TRIMMING

of *Thomas Nashe Gentleman*,
by the high-tituled patron *Don*
Richardo de Medico campo, Barber
Chirurgion to Trinitie Colledge in Cambridge.

Faber quas fecit compedes ipse gestat.

LONDON,
Printed for Philip Scarlet
1597.

To the Learned.

Eme, perlege, nec te precii pœnitebit.

To the simple.

Buy mee, read me through, and thou wilt not repente thee of thy coſt.

To the Gentle Reader.

PR oface gentle Gē-
tlemen, I am forry I haue
no better Cates to prefét
you with: but pardon I
pray you, for this which
I haue heere prouided,
was bred in Lent, and Lent (you know) is
faid of *leane*, becaufe it macerates & makes
leane the bodye: if therefore this dish bee
leane and nothing anfwearable to your ex-
pectation, let it fuffice twas bred in Lent:
neither had it anye time wherein it might
gather anye thinge vnto it felfe to make it
more fat and delightfull. His Epiftle I expected any time thefe three yeares, but this
mine aunfwer *fine fuco loquar*, though it be

To the Reader.

not worthy to bee called the worke of one well spent houre) I haue wrought foorth out of the stolne houres of three weekes: for although occasion hath been offered euer since the Epistle hath been extant, to answere it: yet held in suspence considering the man and matter, whether I should take it vpon mee or no: at last concluding him easily answerable , I haue vndergone it: therefore howsoeuer you see it crept abroad Gentles, receiue it well in worth: Your fauours happily might adde strength vntoit, and stirre vp the faint creeping steps to a more liuely pace: it by hard hap being denied of the progresse, keeping at home hath growne somewhat greater. To tell you what the man is , and the reason of this book, were but triuiall and superfluous, only this, you may call it *The trimming of Thomas Nashe*, wherein hee is described. In trimming of which description, though I haue founde out and fetcht from the mint some few new vvordes to coulor him,

To the Reader.

him, grant me pardon, I thinke them fitte
for him who is so limmed and coullored
vvith all nevv found villanie: for if they bee
etimoligifde, they no vvhit difagree from
his properties. Slender labour hath fuffi-
fed to vveaue this thinne fuperficiall vaile
to couer his crimfon Epistle, and shaddovv
it foorth vnto the vvorld. For as a garment
of too bright a color is too euil an obiect for
the eyes (as is the Sun) & is nothing gazed
after, no not of thofe vvho neuer favv it before: yet nevve things are desired, becaufe
tvvould proue pernicious to their eyes, but
once ore-clovvded and couered vvith a
lavvne vefture, through that it shines & be-
commeth a leffe hurting obiect, and dravvs
the peoples fight after it: fo his Epistle in it
ovvne colour beeing too refplendent and
hurtfull to the readers, is laid apart & is nothing in requeft, for that tvvould proue as a
burning glaffe vnto their eyes, but veftured
vvith this Caule & rare-vvrought garmet, it
lofeth part of it hurting vigour, & therefore
is cald to be feene againe.

Loathed.

Loathed tedioufnes I alfo efchewed as no leffe hurtfull than too bright an obiect: the Booke which he dedicateth to me, is fo tedious,that had I read it through,it fo loathfome would haue vvrought more on mee both vpvvard & downvvard,then 3. drams of pilles: his Epiftle is not behinde hand, to that I might fay as faid *Diogenes* to the men of *Minda*, (vvhofe gates vvere greater in analogicall proportion then their Citie:) O yee men of *Minda*,looke to your Citie,that it flyes not out at your gates: So his booke might well for the largeneffe of the Epiftle haue flowne out at it, and furely I thinke had his book any wings,that is, any queint deuife flying abroad to pleafe withall, it would neuer haue ftaid till this time: therfore I thinke it prouidently done of him (though out of doubt the foole had no fuch drift)to make the gates fo bigge,that when vve haue paffed through the gates, fuppofing all the Cittie to be futable to the ftatelines of them: but after we are entred , finding

ing

To the Reader.

ing our felues meerely guld, and that all the
Cittie is not worth the gates, vvee may the
more readily finde the vvay out of the
Cittie againe, the gates beeing fo great :
and this remedye I founde once vvhen
I tooke my iourney into his Cittie. But
to returne, If this bee not fo vvell fet foorth
as you could vvish it vvere, blame mee not:
for as the Moon being naked & bare, is faid
once to haue gone to her mother, and asked
of her a coat to cloath her: but she anfvve-
red, there could bee no coate made fit for
her, for her inftabilitie, fometime she being
in the ful, and fomtime in the vvane: fo hee
being a man of fo great reuolution, I could
not fit him, for if I had vndertaken to fpeak
of one of his properties, another came into
my mind, & another follovved that, vvhich
bred confufion, making it too little for him:
therefore vvere it not too little, it might be
tvvold be fit, but hovvfoeuer, pardon (Gentlemen) my boldnes in prefenting to your
fauorable viewes this litle & côfufed coate.

Yours in all curtefie, *Richard Lichfield.*

The trimming of Thomas Nashe.

IR, heere is a gentleman at the doore would speake with you. Let him come in. M. *Nashe*! welcome. What, you would be trimd? & I cannot denie you that fauour. Come, sit downe, Ile trim you my selfe. How now? what makes you sit downe so tenderly? you crintch in your buttocks like old father *Pater patria*, he that was father to a whole countrey of bastards. Dispatch, st, boy, set the water to the fire: but sirra, hearke in your eare, first goe prouide me my breakfast, that I goe not fasting about him; then goe to the Apothecarie, and fetch mee some represiue *Antidotum* to put into the bason, to keepe downe the venomous vapors that arise from his infectious excremẽts: for (I tell you) I like not his countenance, I am afraid he labours of the venereall murre.

Muse not (gentle *Thomas*) that I come so roughly vppon you with Sit downe, without anie Dedicatorie Epistle, which (I know) you expected; for that your Epistle (in some wise) brought forth this small Worke: which purposely I omitted, scorning Patronage against you. For if (by an Epistle) I had made some Lord or Knight my Patron, it would haue menaged and giuen courage to you, that (not sufficient of my selfe) I should get some Protector to stand out with you. As in a Cocke-fight, if the Cocke-master takes off his Cocke when they are buckled together, it encourageth the other Cocke (dee-

ming

ming his aduersarie to flye to his Master for refuge): so
that hee crowes foorth the triumph before the victorie.
Therefore forsooth, if for orders sake (that of custome
might be made a necessarie law) you would haue an E-
pistle, I thought it best, respecting the subiect matter, as
neere as possibly I could to patterne it with the like Patron. Then not knowing where to heare of some mis-
creant, polluted with all vices both of bodie & minde :
and viewing ouer all the imprest images of men in the
memoriall cell of my braine, at last I espied your selfe
more liuely ingrauen than the rest, and as it were offring
your selfe to this purpose. Then presently I made choice
of you, that like an asse you might beare your burden, &
patronize your owne scourge, as dooth the silly hedge-
sparrow, that so long fostereth vp the cuckow in her
neast, till at length she bee deuoured of her : or the Vi-
per, that is destroyed of her owne whelpes. All *England* for a Patron. But to this sodaine ioy, (for sodaine
ioy soone ends) this crosse happened ; That knowing it
to bee my duetie to gratulate my Patrone with the first
hereof, but not knowing where to finde you, for that
you (the Worlds Citizen) are heere and there, you may
dine in this place, & goe supperlesse to bed, if you know
where to haue your bed : you maye bee in one prison to
day, and in another to morrow : so that you haue a place
but as a fleeting incorporeall substaunce, circumscribed
with no limits, that of your owne you haue not so much
as one of *Diogenes* his poore cottages. You haue indeed
a *terminus a quo* (as we Logicians speake) but no *terminus ad quem*. Now sir, for the vncertaintie of your man-
sion house, you hauing all the world to keepe Court in,
and being so haunted with an earthquake, that in what
house soeuer you are one daye, you are shaken out the
next, my little Booke might kill three or foure porters,
that

*O elo-
quence.*

*Item for
you.*

Wel put in

*How hard-
ly I leaue
this com-
mon place?*

that muſt run vp and downe *London* to ſeeke you, and at
the laſt might dye it ſelfe for want of ſuccour before it
comes to your hands. Yet it might bee, that in your requeſt you are inſatiable, you will take no excuſe, your
will is your reaſon, nay may not be admitted. Well, it
ſhall be yours: for your Epiſtles ſake, haue at you with
an Epiſtle.

B 2   To

To the polypragmaticall, parasitupocriticall,
and pantophainoudendeconticall Puppie
Thomas Nashe, Richard Leichfield wish-
eth the continuance of that he hath : that is,
that he want not the want of health, wealth,
and libertie.

Nas hum   Mitto tibi Nashum prora N puppi humque carentem.

OD saue you (right gloſſomachicall
Thomas). The vertuous riches, where-
with (as broad ſpread Fame reporteth)
you are indued, though *fama malum*,
(as ſaith the poet) which I confirme :
for that ſhee is *tam ficti pranique tenax,
quam nuncia veri*, as well ſaith Maſter *William Lilly* in
his *Adiecbiua verbalia in ax*. I ſay the report of your rich
vertues ſo bewitched me toward you, that I cannot but
ſend my poore Book to be vertuouſly ſuccoured of you,
that when both yours & my frends ſhall ſee it, they may
(for your ſake) vertuouſly accept of it. But, it may be,
you denie the Epiſtle, the Booke is of you, tho Epiſtle
muſt be to ſome other. I anſwer, you are deſirous of an
Epiſtle. Did not *Caſar* write thoſe things himſelf which
himſelfe did? and did not *Lucius* that golden Aſſe ſpeak
of himſelf which was the Aſſe ? & will not you (though
an

an Affe, yet neither golden nor filuer) patronize that
which others tooke paines to write of you? *Cæfar* and
Lucius for that fhall liue for euer: and fo fhall you, as
long as euer you liue. Go too I fay, he is an ill horfe that
will not carrie his owne prouender. But chiefly I am to
tell you of one thing, which I chufe to tell you of in my
Epiftle, both becaufe of Epiftles fome be denuntiatorie,
as alfo confidering that wife faying elfwhere of the pre-
cife Schoolemafter: If thy frend commit anie enormious offence toward thee, tell him of it in an Epiftle. And
truly this is a great and enormious offence, at which my
choller ftands vpright, neither will I put it vp.   Therefore in fadnes prouide your Lawier, I haue mine, it will
beare as good an action, as if you fhould haue come into another mans houfe, and neuer fay, Hoe God be here:
that is, you wrote a foule Epiftle to mee, and neuer told
me of it before: you might haue faid, By your leaue fir.
I warrant you I write but this fmall Epiftle to you, and I
tell you of it as long before as the Epiftle is long. But
now I remember me, there was no hatred betwen vs
before, and therefore twould be prooued but chaunce-
medley.   Let it euen alone, it cannot be vndone, for a
thing eafely done, neuer can be vndone: and a man may
quickly become a knaue, but hardly an honeft man. And
thus (maleuolent *Tom*) I leaue thee.   From my chamber in *Camb*. to your".

"where cā
you tell?

That is,
that wold
folow thee
euen to the
gallowes.

Yours in loue *vfque ad aras.*

Rich: Lichfield.

B 3   You

YOu see howe louingly I deale with you in my E-
piſtle and tell of your vertues, which (God for-
giue me for it) is as arrant a lye as euer was told : but to
leaue theſe parergaſticall ſpeeches and to come to your
trimming, becauſe I will deale roundly with you, I wil
cut you with the round cut,in which I include two cuts:
Firſt the margent cut : Secondly, the perfect cut : The
margent cut is nothing els but a preparation to the perfect cut, wherby I might more perfectly diſcharge that
cut vpon you,for as in a deep ſtanding poole,the brinks
thereof, which are not vnfitly called the margents being pared away, we may the better ſee thereinto : ſo the
margents which fitly we may terme the brinkes of your
ſtinking ſtanding poole (for it infects the eare as doth
the ſtinking poole the ſmell)being cut away, I may the
better finiſh this perfect cut and rid my ſelfe of you. To
the margent cut. When firſt your Epiſtle came into my
hands, I boldly opened it, and ſcaling the margents of it
I eſpied a ſeely note *quaſi conuerſant about heads.* I ſayd
not a word, but turning ouer a leaſe or twoo more to ſee
if you continued in thoſe ſimple animaduerſions,and indeed I ſaw you to bee no changling,for there I eſpied
barbers knacking of their fingers, & lowſie naperie, as foo-
liſh as the other,*ſemper idem* (thought I)might be your
mot, and ſo you will dye : then I began to marke the
note which you adioyned to your notes that they might
be noted, there toſſing and turning your booke vpſide
downe, when the weſt end of it hapned to be vpward,
me thought your note ſeemed a *D*,ah *Dunce*,*Dolt*,*Dot-*
terell, quoth I, well might it be a *D*.and for my life for
the ſpace of twoo houres, could I not leaue rayling of
thee all in *D*s.

Now to the perfect cut: I cannot but admire you in
well

the tittle you allow me, seeing wee admire monsters as well as vertuous men, and a foole (as oft I haue heard Scholers dispute in mine office) as a monster: other Barbers like not the title, it pleaseth me, and all the Dukes in *Spaine* cannot shew the like, and I thinke that halfe a yeeres study did not bring it out of thy dunsticall hammer-headed scalpe, but thou dost to disgrace mee, and thinkst thy title decketh a Barber, and that a Barber with thy title is as a rotten chamber hangd with cloth of arras, but tis not so: alas thy reading affoords thee not to knowe the ancient and valorous power of Barbers.

I could speake howe they flourished amongst the *Abants*, a fierce and warlike people, and by the Barbers perpolike cunning as it were amending nature and shaping their faces to more austeritie, they became more victorious, as *Plutarch* recordeth in the life of *Theseus*: and young stripplings newly fit for armes, first were brought to *Delphos*, and there offered the first fruites of their haire to *Iupiter*, next him the Barbers were serued and they cut them, and were as *Ioues* Vises to make them fit for warre. They flourished before with the *Arabians*, the *Mysians*, the *Dacians*, the *Dalmatians*, the *Macedonians*, the *Thracians*, the *Seruians*, the *Sarmacians*, the *Valachians* and the *Bulgarians*, as saith *Pollidorus Virgil*: afterward *Alexander* entertained into his campes Barbers as the spurres and whetstones of his armies.

Dionisius that blood-thirstie Tyrant that feared no peeres, stoode alwaies in feare of Barbers, and rather would haue his hayre burnt off, than happen into the Barbers handes.

Therefore in a Barbers shop (as *Platarche* reporteth) where some fewe were talking of the Tyrany

of

of the tyger *Dionyſius*. What (ſaid the Barber) are you talking of King *Dionyſius*, whome within theſe two or three daies I muſt ſhaue? When *Dionyſius* heard of this, he gate the Barber ſecretly to be put to death, for feare of after-claps. The Barbers Chaire is the verie Royall-Exchange of newes, Barbers the "head of all Trades. I could ſpeake of their excellencie, for that a mans face (the principall part of him) is committed onely to Barbers. All trades adorne the life of man, but none (except Barbers) haue the life of man in their power, and to them they hold vp their throates readie.

None but Barbers meddle with the head.

If they be happie, whom pleaſure, profit and honor make happie, then Barbers with great facilitie attaine to happines. For pleaſure, if they be abroad, they are ſoght too of the beſt Companions, Knights and Eſquires ſend for them : if at home and at worke, they are in pleaſing conference ; if idle, they paſſe that time in life-delighting muſique. For profite, a Barber hath liuing in all parts of *England :* he hath money brought in as due as rents, of thoſe whom he neuer ſaw before. For honour, Kings and ruling Monarchs, (to whom all men crouch with cap in hand and knee on ground) onely to Barbers ſit barehead, and with bended knees. But for all this, thou ſpareſt not to raile on Barbers (as on all others) : & being full of botches and byles thy ſelfe, ſpueſt forth thy corruption on all others : but I nought reſpect it, thy raylings rather profite mee. For (as *Antiſthenes* was wont to ſay) a man might as well learne to liue well of his ill-willing & abuſiue enemies, as of his honeſt frends; of theſe, by following their vertues, of the others by eſchuing their actions, by ſeeing the effects that followed thoſe actions in his enemies : and as *Telephus* (beeing wounded, and deſtitute of a ſauing remedie at home) went euen to his enemies and ſworne foes, to get ſome

ſoue-

souerraigne medicine, so if of my friendes I could not learne temperance, I might learne of thee by seeing the effectes of thy cankered conuicious tongue, for by that thou art brought into contempt, thy talking makes thee bee accounted as a purse that cannot bee shutte, and as an house whose doore standes alwayes open, and as that open purse contayneth no siluer, and in that house is nothing worthie the taking away, so out of thy mouth proceedeth nothing but noysome and ill-sauered vomittes of railinges : Wherefore draw together the stringes, and locke vp the doore of thy mouth, and before thou speakest such ill corrupted speeches againe let it be lifted of the hingelles, rule I say that little and troubelsome Vermin that smal tongue of thine, which in some is not the smallest parte of vertue, but in thee the greatest Arte of vice, not vnlike the Purple fish which whilest she gouernes her tongue well, it getteth her foode and hunteth after her praye, but when shee neglect it, it bringeth her destruction, and she is made her selfe a pray vnto the fisher, so that in that small parcell all vertue and vice lyes hidden, as is recorded of *Kias* whom king *Amasis* commaunding to sende home the best and most profitable meate from the market, hee sent home a tongue, the king demaunding a reason, hee answered that of a tongue came many profitable and good speeches, and this tongue thou hast not : Then the king sent him to buy the woorst and most vnprofitable meate, and he likewise bought a tongue, the king also asking the reason of this, from nothing (sayde he) issueth worse venome then from the tongue, and this tongue thou hast, and this tongue crosse with the barre of reason, lest thou seeme more foolish then those geese in *Cilicia*, which when the flie in the night time by the hill *Taurus,*

C   that

that is poffeft of Eagles, are fayde to gette ftones into ther mouthes by which as by a bridle they raine in their cryinges, and fo quietly paffe the greedie talentes of the Eagles: but alas why inuect I fo againft thy tongue? *lingua* a *lingeudo*, and you knowe wee vfe alwayes to like in, and fo thou fhouldeft keepe in thy poyfon: or a *ligando* which is to binde, and fo thou fhouldeft binde vp and not difperfe abroad that ranker in thee: thy tongue doth but in dutie vtter that which is committed vnto it, and nature hath fet before it a double bull-woorke of teeth to keepe in the vagrant wordes which ftraying abroade and beeing furprifed may betray the whole cittie, and the vpper bull-woorke fometimes ferues for a percullis, which when any rafcallie woorde hauing not the watch-worde, that is, *reafon*, fhall but enter out of the gates, is prefently lette downe and fo it cuttes it of before it woorketh wracke to the whole Caftell: therefore I muft of neceffitie find out another caufe of thine infected fpeech, and now I haue founde it, fie on thee, I fmell thee, thou haft a ftinkinge breath, but a ftinking breath (fome fay) commeth of foule teeth, and if it bee fo, wafh thy teeth Tom, for if thou wouldeft drawe foorth good and cleane wordes out of thy mouth, thou wouldeft wafhe thy teethe as euerie tapfter that goeth to drawe good beare will wafhe the potte before hee gooeth: but it may bee the filth hath fo eaten into thy teeth that wafhinge cannot gette it away, then doe as that venome-bitinge beaft that Nile-breede Crocodile, which to purge her teethe of thofe fhiuered reedes that are wreathed betweene by feedinge in the water, commeth tot the fhoore, and there gapinge fuffereth fome friendly bird with-

Marke this fecret allegorie.

ous

out daunger to creepe into her mouth , and with
her bill to picke away the troubling reedes : fo
come you but to fome fhoore , and Ile bee that
Trochilus , Ile picke your teeth and make a cleane
mouth , or Ile picke out toungue and all , but of
this ftinkinge breath I fpeake not . *Tædet anima*
fayth the Comedian , and this I meane not meaning as hee meant , for hee meant a ftinkinge
breath , but by *anima* I meane the forme by which
thou art, what thou art , by which alfo thy fenfes
woorke , which giueth vfe to all thy faculties and
from which all thy actions proceede , and this *anima* if thou termift a breath , this breath ftinketh
and from this breath (as little riuers flowe from a
fountaine) all thy woordes flowe foorth and the
fountaine beeing corrupted (as you knowe) like-
wife all the leffer riuers needes muft bee corrupted,
and this *anima* , this breath or fountayne thou muft
cleanfe , but howe to cleanfe this breath it paffeth
my cunninge to tell , fot thoughe (as I am a Cir-
urgion) I coulde picke your teeth , for the other
ftinkinge breath , yet this I durft not meddle with,
this hath neede of a metaphifition , and lette it
fuffice for mee rudely to take vppe the bucklers and
laie them downe againe , onely to tune the Lute,
but to leaue to the more cunning to playe there-
on , Count it enough for mee that am but an ad-
uincte to a Scholler , that haue nothinge of my
felfe but what I gleane vppe at the difputation of
fome Schollers in myne office , let it bee fuffici-
ent for mee (I fay) onely to tell the reafon of this
ftinkinge breath , and to leaue to more founde Philofophers to determine and fet downe the remedie of it,
but nowe it may bee *teipfum nofcis*, you fmell your

Trochilus

philofophy

*How I be-
wich thee
with fa-
cunditie.*

owne

C 2

owne breath, and finde it to bee so intoxicated with
poyson that vnlesse you haue present helpe you are
quite vndone, you perish vtterly, and knowing me to
be a man of such excellent partes, yea of farre better
partes then *In speach bee these eight partes*, are very in-
stant with me to vnbinde the bundell which I gathered at disputations, and giue you some remedie for
this stinkinge breath: loe howe vertue in the friend
casteth foorth her beames euer vpon her enemie, I
am ouercome, blushingly I vndertake it, and like a
bashfull mayde refuse, yet deigne you that fauour,
then marke, first goe get some strong hempe, and
worke it and temper it so long together till therearise
out of it an engine which wee call *Capistrum*, then
carry this *Capistrum* to some beame that lyeth a crosse,
for none else will serue, when it must bee straynde
and the one ende of it fasten to the beame, and one
the other make a noose of as rounde a figure as you
can for the roundest figure is the most retentiue, let
the noose bee alwayes readie to slide, for mans
breath is slipperie, then when euerie thing is fitted,
boldly put through thy heade, then worke the *Capistrum* ouer newe agayne, swinge vppe and downe
twice or thrice that it may be well strainde, and so
in short time your olde breath will bee gone, dis-
payre not yet man, *probatum est*, olde Æson was
deade a while but reuiued agayne and liued many
a yeare after, but marke, nowe to the pynche, if
Platoes trasmigration holde, (which some menne
holde that the *anima* and breathes of men that bee
deade doe fleete into the bodyes of other menne
which shall liue, then I holde that some breath seeing thy younge bodie without an *anima*, and twould
bee harde lucke if some breath or other should not

be

Ha ha a rage borro wed from your owne dunghil!.

A medi cine for a stinking breath.

be yet ſtraying about for a body , their being con-
tinually ſo many let looſe at Tiburne, I ſay , ſome
vnbeſpoken vagrant breath wil goe in and poſſeſſe thy
body : nowe if this remedie helpe not ſurely thou art
vnrecurable , If alſo thy newe breath happen to be as
ſtinking as thy olde , thou wilt neuer haue a ſweete
breath in this worlde nor then neither . And thus
much of my title.

You knowe or at the leaſt ought to knowe that
writers ſhoulde eſhewe lyes as Scorpions , but your
lyes that you deuiſd of one are the greateſt parte of
the matter of your Epiſtle, as, *My ſhoppe in the towne,*
the teeth that hange out at my Windowe , my painted
may-poole, with many others which fill vp roome in
the Epiſtle in aboundant manner, and which are nothing elſe but meere lyes and fictions to yeeld the matter, whereby I perceiue howe threede-bare thou art
waxen , howe barren thy inuention is , and that thy
true amplifying vaine is quite dryed vppe . Repent,
repent, I ſay, and leaue of thy lying which without
repentance is very haynous , that one lye I make of Pag : 6,
thee in this booke is preſently waſhed away with repentance . An other lye I cannot but tell you off,
which you clappe in my teeth in the very beginning
of your Epiſtle , which nothinge greeueth mee for
that I ſuppoſe it to bee committed of ignorance ,
that is you tell mee that you come vpon mee with
but a dicker of Dickes , but you come vppon mee
with ſeuenteene or eighteene Dickes , whereby I ſee
thy ignorance in the Greeke tongue, thou knoweſt not
what a dicker is , a dicker is but ten of any thing, for it
commeth of the Greeke worde δέϟρα which is by in-
terpretation, Ten.   *de ka*

Thou obiecteſt that olde *Tooly* and I differed , I

confesse it, I am a man alone, I scorne such ragged rent-foorth speech, yet thou mayeft well praye for the duall number, thou scabbed, scalde, lame, halting adiectiue as thou art, in all thy guiles, thou neuer hadest that guile as alone to get thee one crust of breade: no, I knowe not who had a hande with you in this seely Epistle, goe too, hee is not a minister, he hadde but small reason for it: againe, you remember the time when your fellowe *Lusher* and you lay in cole-harbour together, when you had but one payre of breeches betweene you both, but not one penie to blesse you both, and howe by course hee woore the breeches one day, and went cunny-catching about for victuals, whilest you lay in bedde, and the next day you wore the breeches to goe begge whilest he lay in bed, for all the worlde like two bucketes in one well, nowe suppose, when *Lusher* wore the breeches, that then thou shouldest haue beene carryed to pryson where nowe thou art, verily I thinke thou shouldest haue escaped prison for want of breeches, or suppose that at that time thou shouldest haue beene hanged, I cannot but thinke that the want of a payre of breeches woulde haue beene better to thee then thy necke-verse, for the hange-man would haue his breeches, no fee, no lawe: but put case that with much adoe, by greate extraordinarie fauour some good hang-man had done thee this last benifitte, that thou mightest neuer troble him agayne, and shoulde haue giuen thee thy hanginge francke and free (as indeede happy for thee had it bene if this good hap had hapned, for then thou shouldst not haue liued thus miserably in this vaine and wicked worlde) I say plainely, put case thou haddest beene hanged, the hangman not sticking with thee for thy breeches, then *Chacon* would haue come vpon
you

you for his ferry-penny, fie out, money and breeches as ill as a rope and butter, for if one flippe the
other holde, with him no *naulum* no waftage, and then
thou haddeft beene in worfe cafe then euer thou wert:
thus you fee how the want of a payre of breeches might
haue been the meanes to haue made thee efcape prifon,
death and vtter damnation: and O thrife happy *Lufher*
that fhouldft haue beene away with the breeches at that
happy time, but when thou wert in thy chiefeft pride,
if thou hadft but lent out one payre of breeches thou
fhouldft haue beene thus happy.

Prayfe from the praife-worthy, and hee is not
prayfed whofe prayfer deferueth not prayfe, therefore in thefe places of the Epiftle where thou pray-
feft mee, I take my felfe moft to bee difpraifed for
that thou the prayfer art worthie no praife, for how
foeuer thou leade in a fooles paradife, like the fifhe
cald a muge, which is fayde to feede herfelfe with
her owne fnotte for thereof fhee takes her name, thou
feadeft thy-felfe with felf-conceite that whatfoeuer
commeth from thee is the verie quinteffence of true
witte, and that all thy ribaldrie that euer thou
fettft forth, exceeded in pleafing mirth, that fo thou
haft imbraced true *Minerua*, when as (God knowes)
thou art as farre deceiued as euer was poore *Ixion*,
that imbraced a cloude in fteade of *Iuno*, or that
guld-god moftrous accadian *Pan*, who in fteade
of that fweete Nimphe *Syrinx* fumpt a bunche of
reedes: yet I muft confeffe thou hafte fomething,
thou art as a bundell of ftrawe that beeing fett on
fire confumes it felfe all in fmoke, but no warm-
neffe commeth from it, fo thou haft no true fire in
thee, all fmoother, no thing that can warme a man,
thou art as many Ciphers without an I, which they

*Mucus
fnotte.*

C 4   wan-

wanting are of them felues nothing, and thou haft
much apparencie of witte which is as Ciphers, but thou
haft not this fame I, Iota is wanting to thy Ciphers,
thou haft not one iot nor title of true witte, againe,
as fome fouldiers that were at *Cales* breaking into a
fhoppe for pillage, and there feeing many great fackes
readie truffed vppe, they with great ioy made haft
away with them, and fo with light hartes carryed
away their heauie burdens, and when they brought
them into the ftreetes, opening them to fee their
booties, founde in fome of them nought but redde
cappes, of which afterward they made ftore of fires,
and in the reft nought but earthen pitchers, chaffen-
diſhes and pifpottes, and fuch like : fo whofoeuer fhall
fee thee truffed vppe and in thy clothes, might
happily take thee for a wife young man, but when
thou fhalt be opened, that is, when he fhall fee but fome
worke of thine, he fhall finde in thee nought but raf-
callitie and meere delufions, and for this caufe thou
mayeft be cald the very *Choræbus* of our time, of whom
the prouerbe was rayfde, more foole then *Choræbus*,
who was a feely ideot, but yet had the name of a wife
man, for he might be cald *Choræbus quaſi chori Phos*,
the light of euery company into which hee came, fo
thou haft onely the name of a wife man and that is
Nafhe, O wife name, I praye let mee chriften you a
newe and you fhall bee called *Choroebus quaſi chori
bos*, the very bull-heade of all he ttroope of pamphleters : thou goeft about to gather ieftes and to barrell
them vp into thine ale-howfe index, that when occa-
fion fhall ferue thou mighteft be a *Democritus* alwayes
to laugh thy felfe or to caufe others to laugh by the
ideotifme. Thus to conclude, as *Daphne* chaftitie was
turnd into a laurell tree, and fo kept her chaftitie, euen

fo

ſo I wiſh that for thy wit thou mightſt bee turnd into an
aſſe, that ſo thou mightſt keepe thy wit to thy ſelfe, and
not defile the world withall. But this thou ſcornſt, and
wilt prooue that thou haſt a good wit, and thus ſubmiſ-
ſiuely in eloquence, to make vs beleeue thee , at the firſt
word thou beginſt ; Nature, that neuer wont to be vne-
quall in her gifts, with mee hath broke her wont, and indowed me with a dowrie aboue the reſt of her children :
but euerie commoditie hath his diſcommoditie, and we
cannot alwaies pleaſe all ; and though all my books did
not take as I wiſhed they ſhould, yet moſt of them did
take, as *Piers Pennileſſe*, and others which I will not
name, to auoyd ſuſpition of vainglorie *Argu* that had
an hundred eyes ſometime ſlept, or els hee had not dyed
for it : and when *Mercurie* came, hee had no power to
hold ope his eyes. O fine ſpeech ! By this I gather, that
thou confeſſeſt thy ſelfe to be *Argus*, and me *Mercury*:
and if you be *Argus*, hold ope your eyes with a pox to ye,
I meane yee no harme yet, yet I pipe not to you : but I
thinke it will be my lucke to be as ill a ſcourge to you, as
euer *Mercurie* was to *Argus*. But if you will diſpute
and prooue that you haue a good wit, away with your
confuſed bibble babble binde vp your Arguments into
Syllogiſmes and I will anſwere you directly. Content
ſay you, and thus you begin. If my fame be ſpred far
abroad, & all the Countrey confirme that I haue a good
wit, then tis true that I haue a good wit : But the firſt pro-
poſition is true, therefore I haue a good wit. I anſwer,
Poore and illiterate Opponent, to contex no firmer argument againſt ſo firme a Logician as I am. A double
Reſponſe or Aunſwere extempore I can affoord you.
Firſt, though your name bee blazed abroad, it followes
not that you ſhould haue a good wit : for as an emptie
veſſell will ſound farre that hath nothing in it ; ſo you

may

may cracke your selfe abroad, and get to be reported the man you are not.

Secondly, I graunt that you are famous, and that the Countrey reports you wise. Sententiously I aunswere, that by a figure the Countrey is taken here for the common rout onely : for none that can but write and read will euer agree to it ; and *turba malum argumentum*, as much as to saye, the troublesome Commons assertion, neuer goes for currant. Thus leauing no hole for you to creepe in with a second Obiection, you betake you to your second Argument.

If my wit (saye you) were not excellent and vnaunswerable, manie who are accounted to haue good wits, (to whom I haue oft giuen perticular occasion) would haue answered mee : but they haue not answered mee, therefore my wit is excellent. Therefore I wyll aunswere thee.

I would to God thou & I were to dispute for the best Mayorship in *Spaine*, faith thou mightest euen cast thy cap at it. Doost thou not know that the Lion scornes combate with the bace ? Wise-men (though mooued) will not worke reuenge on euerie obiect ? and the more stately oake, the more hardly set on fire ? More plainly in a similitude, the like reason is to bee gathered of the nettles.

Euen as the nettle keepeth her leafe cleanest, for that no man purgeth his post-pendence (there your nose *Thomas*) with it ; not because they cannot, but because it would sting them if they should, and so for that small goodturne, it would worke them a more displeasure : so thou art suffered to be quiet, and not wrote against, not for that thou canst not bee aunswered, but that by aunswering thee they should but giue more fodder to thy poison, put more casting to thy gorge ; and hee that intends
tends

tends to meddle with dung, muſt make account to defile his fingers.

Thus thou art quite put downe, thou art drawne drie: me thinkes I perceiue thee wiſh for ſome Moderatour, that ſhould crie ; *Egregie Naſh* (or, you great aſſe) *ſatisfeciſti officium tuum.* And now for want of a Moderatour, my ſelfe (for fault of a better) will ſupplye that roome, and determine of our Diſputation. And herein it ſhall not bee amiſſe, (the Queſtion ſo requiring, and you alſo requiring it in that place of your Epiſtle, where you lay wit to my charge) firſt to tell what a good wit is. And whereas thou burthenſt me to ſay, that *much extraordinarie deſcant cannot be made of it :* thou lyeſt. For how vniuſt were mens wits, not to affoord vs extraordirie deſcant of that, which giueth vs deſcant for euerye thing?

A good wit (therefore) is an affluent ſpirit, yeelding inuention to praiſe or diſpraiſe, or anie wayes to diſcourſe (with iudgement) of euerie ſubiecte. Miſtake me not (I pray you) and think not that I thinke all thoſe to haue good wits, that will talke of euerie ſubiect, and haue an oare (as we ſay) in euerie mans boate : for manie fooles doo ſo, and ſo dooſt thou. Theſe talke not with iudgement : they be like the Fellow, who ſwearing by God, and one ſtanding by, correcting him, ſaid; Fie on thee how thou talkeſt. What skills it ſaid hee, ſo long as I talke of God? So I ſay, thou careſt not how without iudgement thou talkeſt on euerie thing.

A good wit is it that maketh a man, and hee is not a man, that hath not a good wit. The verie brutiſh and ſauage beaſts haue wit. Oxen and Aſſes by theyr wit chooſe out the beſt Paſture to feed in, and thou art no better : for diuers men will ſay, and eſpecially Northeren men, to one that dooth anie thing vnhandſomely,

whaten

what an a Nash it is, for what an asse it is, and an asse all
men know hath not a good wit.

Thus (by these descriptions) the definitiue sentence
of my determination is this ; *Nashe*, thou hast not a
good wit, thou art a silly fellow, and more silly than Syr
Thomas of *Carleton*, who beeing a little sicke, and the
bell tolling to haue him goe read Seruice, the Clarke of
the Parish going to him, and telling him that the bell
toalde for him, meaning to goe Read, he went presently
and made his Will, because the bell toalde for him: and
so doo thou plye thee, make thy Will, and dye betimes
before thou beest killd, for thine owne wit will kill thee:
and call you that a good wit that kills a man ? All the
Wisemen of *Greece* and *Gotam* neuer came to the miserie that thy good wit hath brought thee too. My
minde presageth the great confusion that thy good wit
will bring vppon thee. For as the Cammell that (come
hee into neuer so cleare a Fountaine) cannot drinke of
the Water, till hee hath royled and fowled it with his
feete : so whatsoeuer thy wit goeth about, it first defiles
it, and so brings destruction to thine owne bodie. Thy
wit, thy wit *Tom*, hath roddes in pisse for thee, twil
whip thee, twill worke thine ouerthrow, twill quite de-
stroye thee : *Acteon* (as wise a man as you) no
wayes could escape it, for all his loue to his hounds,
and swift flight when he saw their selues, but was deuoured of his owne dogs.

But why then (maist thou say) doo I oppose my
selfe against an Asse, seeing now I doo no more than all
could doo, for all the beasts in the field can insult and
triumph ouer the silly Asse, as well the creeping Snayle
to her power as the fiercest Tyger. *Asinus a sedendo*,
because euerie Childe can ride an asse : therefore tis rather a reproachfull shame for mee to meddle with thee,

and

and by that I get more difcredit then the two Gods
got difhonors that confpired the downe-fall of one feely, weake, vnable woman. The reafon is, I onely am
left to tell thee thou art an Affe, and if thou fhouldft not
be tolde it, thou wouldft not beleeue that thou art an
Affe. Therefore nowe at length knowe thine owne
ftrength, and knowing that thou art but feeble and
haft no ftrength, blufh and be afhamed, and then thou
fhalt fee that all the Country hath feene thy ignorance,
though kept it in filence, and howe this many a yeere
thou haft guld them, but they (gentle minded au-
ditors) ftill, ftill, expecting better tooke all in good
part, whilft thou like a cowardly vnskilfull horfeman
mounted on a iade, coruetteft and fheweft thy Crankes
among a company of valorous famous captaines whofe
ftirrop thou art not worthy to holde : alight and liften
vnto me, and I euen I, that neuer till now was acquain-
ted with the preffe, and acknowledge my felfe farre vn-
fit for thofe thinges thou profeffeft, I (I fay) will read
thee a Lecture, harken, in my gibbridg (as thou termft
it) I wil confter thee this fhorte diftich which though it
wants an author wants no authoritie.

Thaida te credis duxiffe, fed illa Diana eft,

Namque Acætoeneum dat tibi Caura caput

Ingennoufly thou thee complainft an Irus poore to be,

But thou art Midas for thou art an Affe as well as he.

Or thus.

Some fayes Nafhe is lafciuious, but I fay he is chaft,

For he by chacing after whores, his beard away hath chaft.

Otherwife.

Who faies Nafh riots day & night, about the ftreets doth lye

For he in prifon day and night in fetters faft doth lye.

Againe.

You fay I am a foole for this, and I fay you fay true,

Then

Then what I say of you is true, for. babes and fooles say true.

Now I giue not euery word their litterall sence, and
by that you may see how I presume of your good wit,
to see if by allusions you can picke out the true meaning, but I vse a more plaine demonstration and apply
it to your selfe : for if you will vnderstand any thing a
right, you must euer apply it to your selfe . It may bee
thou likest not these verses for that they want riming
words, and I ende both the verses with one word : no,
Tom, noe, thinke not so, bewray not so thy poetry, for
that distich is best contriued , and moste elegant that
endes both verses with one word if they import a diuers
sence : but now I see thou art no versifier, thou hast only
a prose tongue, & with that thou runst headlong in thy
writing with great premeditation had before, which a-
ny man would suppose for the goodnes to be extempore, and this is thy good wit : come, I say, come learne of
me, Ile teach thee howe to pot verses an houre together.

Thou nothing doubtest (as thou sayest) of the *patro-*
nage & safe conduct of thy booke, and indeed thou needest
not doubt for I neuer ment it harme, but alwayes wisht
it might safely passe by me : yet as I was patron to it, I
could not but read some of it, but I thinke if I had read
it through twould haue poisoned me, it stunke so abho-
minablye : therefore all the while I was reading of it
holding my nose, fye, out said I, had I but knowne this
Cockatrice whilst twas in the shell, I would haue broken it, it neuer should haue beene hatcht by my patronage : but tis no matter , thy eye-beames will re-
flect vpon thy selfe, and will be burning glasses to thine
owne eyes.

And so in a fury (the countries comming downe vp-

                                                    on

on me) I like a ſtout patron out of all the countries that
preſt me ſore, chalenged out the moſt valiant warrier
of them all, *Monſeir Aiax* to ſingle combate, him I o-
uercame, and of him I got ſafe conduct, and hee hath
promiſed ſafe conduct to all commers of that race,
and moreouer, hee as an other patron hath got-
ten for them all ſafe conduct from hence to *Eely* by
water.

The good admonition thou giueſt mee, that is, to
commence, I thankfully take and willingly would vn-
dergoe, had I but one with whome I might keep mine
acts.

As for mine anſwere I nothing doubt, that is kept (as
I hope) with credit, but my replie is it I ſtand on, I can
get none to anſwere me, alas, thou art not able, neyther
fit, for thy want of a beard taketh away halfe the ſubiect
of our diſputation, not that I ſay a beard would make
thee wiſe and ſo by that thou ſhouldſt be fit to diſpute,
but becauſe in what Arte thou wouldſt haue mee commence, in that I would diſpute with thee: therefore ſuppoſe I ſhould demaund of thee the reaſon why thou
haſt ſo much haire on thy head, and ſo thinne or rather almoſt none at all on thy face? thou couldſt not
queintly anſwere, becauſe the haire on thy head is
twenty yeeres elder then that on thy beard, nor in
naturall reaſon, becauſe the braine ſeated in the head
yeeldeth more moyſture about it then any way downeward, by which moyſture haire commeth, but thou
haſt too moiſt a braine that cannot holde and remember theſe thinges, or rather thou haſt too hard
and drye a braine and ſo theſe thinges were neuer impreſt into it.

But

But this is thine anſwere, tis Gods will it ſhould bee ſo,
thou wert neuer borne to haue a beard : tis true indeed,
thus thou mighteſt anſwere to all the arguments in the
worlde : but the want of a beard makes thee thus
colde in anſwering, for a beard is a ſigne of a ſtrong
naturall heate and vigour, but the true anſwere is, thou
ſeekeſt too many wayes to caſt out thine excrementes,
thou art too effeminate and ſo becomſt like a woman
without a beard. Againe, if I ſhould demaund of thee
why the haire of a mans head groweth downeward and
not vpward, *idem reuolueres*, this would bee thine anſwere, becauſe it pleaſeth nature. Doſt thou not know
that haire is the couer of the head? and therefore if it
will couer it muſt lye downe , and doe not all the parts
of a man growe downeward , though the whole man
growes vpwards? And therefore the Philoſophers ſay
that a man turned downeward is a plant, that as a plant
hath all her bowghes, branches and leaues growe vpward, ſo all the partes of a man are vpwarde when hee
ſtandeth on his head, as his feete, legs, armes, noſe, fingers and the reſt : but in faith thou turnd vpward or
downeward art but a plant or ſtocke to bee ignorant
in thoſe thinges : why I maruell of what Art thou
didſt Commence Batchelor , if I had but the queſtion
that thou hadſt at thy ſophiſters Act, I would diſpute
on that : but nowe I ſee I cannot commence for want
of an anſwerer , and I ſcorne to keepe myne acts *in
tenebris.*

In this thy trimming, thou being ſo fit for it , I will
worke a wonder on thee, and I will holde any man a
wager that I will performe it, that is, whilſt I am waſh-
ing you I will requeſt your *conniuence* and put my ſelfe
to *conniuence*, and ſh ue you quite through and when
I haue done you ſhall not be a haire the worſe you may
make

make a riddle of the same if you will, but I will doe it, and when I haue done, raising my selfe on my tiptoes, I will so hunt thee for my pay, that thou shouldst bee in worse case then the Beuer, who bites off his stones and layes them in the way for the hunter: for which other-wise he should be hunted to the death, I thinke verily and in my conscience, *I should breake thy head and not*   *Leaning* *giue the rest againe.*   *on a iest.*

Thou rude wretch, thou wilt be so *cosmologiz'd*, if thou beest catcht heere, for calling our Masters of Arte first *Stigmaticall*, that is burnt with an hot Iron, didst thou euer know any of our Masters of Arts burnt with any I-rons? then thou callest them *sinckanters*, which is a pro-per Epithite vnto thy selfe, for *Sinckanter* commeth of *sincke* and *antrum* a hole, and as all the puddle and filth in the channell, still runnes all along till it comes to a hole or *antrum*, and there it sinckes in: so all wickednes and abhord villany still straying abroad and seeking for an *antrum*, at last it findes thee which art the very sincke and center where it restes. And surely if thou shouldst haue termed me so, I neuer would haue suffered it vnre-uenged, for as the *Torpedo* being caught and layd on the ground, striketh a torpour and numbnes into the hand of him that doth powre but water on her: so, I doe not thinke but that in thy Epistle thou calledst me but *Dick*, which is my name contract, and other adiuncts which in their owne nature are neither good nor bad, the very re-membrance of me stroke such a feare and numbnes in-to thy ioyntes, that yet thou shakest as not dispossest of that fearefull feauer. I will stirre thee vp and make thee seething hot, and when thou art in thy heate, I will then quell thee by moouing of thee more and more, as when a pot seetheth if we lade it and mooue the liquor vp and down, euen while it seetheth, wee shall make it quiet.

E   Thou

Thou little wottest of what a furious spirite I am, for I keeping among such spirits in this place, as thou sayst, am my selfe become a spirit, and goe about with howling cries with my launce in my hand to tortour thee, and must not returne home, till *Ignatius*-like thou shalt be carbonadoed, and I shall carrie on my launce-point thy bones to hang at my shop windowe, in steed of a cronet of rotten teeth, as the trophies of my victorie: and this shalbe done, commest thou neuer so soone into my swinge.

Spirit walks.

Therefore keep out of my hant, I haue a walke, thou maist be blasted before thou commest neere my walke, if thou dost but looke backe and see mee in my walke, thy necke will stand awry, thy mouth distorted, thy lips vgly wrested, and thy nose hang hooke-wise. But rather I take thee to be a spirit, for that I talking with thee all this while, cannot haue a glance on thee.

But

But fee, what art thou heere? *lupus* in *fabula*, a lop in a chaine? Nowe firra haue at you, th'art in my fwinge. But foft, fetterd? thou art out againe: I cannot come neere thee, thou haft a charme about thy legges, *no man meddle with the Queenes prifoner*, now therefore let vs talke freendlye, and as *Alexander* fayd to hys Father *Phillip*, who beeing forely wounded in the thigh in fight, and hardly efcaping death, but could

not

not goe on the ground without halting, bee of good
courage father, come foorth that euery ſtep thou ſets
on the ground may put thee in minde of thy manly courage & vertue: ſo ſay I to thee, *Naſhe* come forth, be not
aſhamed of thy ſelfe, ſtretch out thy legs that euery ſtep
thou goeſt, thy ſhackles crying clinke, may remember &
put thee in minde of all thy goodnes and vertue: I am
glad to ſee thee in this proſperitie , thou neuer wert ſo
rich as now, thou neuer hadſt ſo much money as would
buy ſo faire a payre of fetters: in very deed thou art
beholding to thy keeper that will truſt thee with ſo
faire a payre of fetters, neither would he if hee had thee
not by the legge: but nowe thou art in good caſe, thou
art no vagabond, now thou ſerueſt a Maſter, and haſt a
houſe to goe to, and a coutch to lye in , thou muſte bee
thriuing and prouident where thou art, and twill bee a
good ſauing for thee, now thou haſt a clog at thy heele
as the prouerbe is, thou muſt learne of *Aeſops* dog to do
as he did : that is, thou muſt crinch vp thy ſelfe round in
thy couch all winter time and dreame of a goodly large
chamber, faire lodgings and ſoft beds , and in the Summer time thou muſt ſtretch out thy ſelfe, lye all abroad
ſnoring vpon thy couch , and thinke that ſilly lodging
(ſeeing thou feeleſt no cold) a ſtately chamber built of

Holes in   free ſtone, layd out with ſtately bay windowes for to
the top.   take the ayre at. But what neede I tell thee of theſe
thinges? thou knoweſt better then I howe to lye in
pryſon , for what a ſhame were it elſe for thee, that
haſt many a day agoe beene free of all the pryſons in
London, nowe to learne thine occupation? thou art a
iourney-man long ſince , I doe not thinke but that
thou art able to ſet ope ſhop in that trade, for if thou weꝛt
but a nouice in it , this deere yeere would quite kill
thee.

But

But say, how doſt thou for victualls, doo not they of thy old acquaintance helpe thee? if euer thou hadſt true friend, now let him ſhow himſelfe, for a frend is tried in aduerſitie: and though the Romanes were wont to ſay, that a true frend was but the ſalt and ſauce of a banquet; yet I ſay, that a true Frend to thee muſt be ſalt, ſauce, bread, and all the meate beſide. But thou haſt neuer a true Frend, yet thou haſt enough of thoſe frends, that would be ſauce to thy meate; that is, if thou couldſt bid them to a ſupper, they would come to eate vp thy meat, and ſawce it with fine talke. But (God knowes) thou haſt no need of thoſe frends, thou couldeſt bee ſauce to thine owne meate. Fie on frendſhip, what is become of it? not one drop nor crum of frendſhip betweene them all? A true Frend (as they ſay) were more neceſſarie than water and fire: for vnles hee come and call for it, thou canſt not haue ſo much as fire and water; that is, a fire with a cuppe of ſmall drinke by it to nouriſh thy bodie. What is become of thoſe true Frends *Damon* and *Pythias*, *Caſtor* and *Pollux*, *Pylades* and *Oreſtes*, *Niſus* and *Euriolus*, *Perithous* & *Theſeus*, whom death it ſelfe could neuer ſeperate? Dead? Then *loue* raiſe ſome deadly tyrant to maſſacre that cancred brood of thy companions, that leaue their ieſter deſolate in the winter of his affliction. I curſe them with more vehemencie, becauſe I ſee ſome hope in thee, in that thou now ſeemeſt ſimply to betake thee to the truth. For whereas thou wert wont to cracke and brag abroad, and indeuouredſt to ſhew, that ther was no learning in which thou wert not expert, and how that thou wert indowed with plentie of the liberall Sciences; which thou knoweſt to be nothing ſo: now thou recanteſt, and in ſimple truth ſaiſt, thou haſt no learning, no not ſo much as one of the liberall Sciences. Which thou ſhoweſt vnto vs by comming foorth in thy

fetters,

fetters, for none of the sciences are bond-slaues, or kept
in chaines, they are called liberall *quasi libers* because
they make men free. If these are not sufficient motiues
for thee, happily let this moue thee, that by thy proficiencie in philosophy since thou camst into prison , thou
hearing of *Aesop* that dwelt in a tub; of *Anaxagoras*, who,
in prison wrote his especiall booke *Of the quadrature of
the Circle*: of *Socrates*, who in prison studied Philosophy,
and wrote verses, and yet (as *Cardan* saith) slept sweetly,
so as *Socrates* gaue more light to the prison , than the
prison gaue darknes to *Socrates*: And lastly of him that
put out his owne eyes, and so eclipst himself of the sight
of the world, that he might haue a more cleere insight
into the light of nature: keep thou thy self still in prison,
eclispe thee from the sight of the world, gaze onely on
thy selfe, that so thou more cleerely, seeing thine owne
deformed nature , mightst labour to reforme it, and
bring thy selfe into light againe. But (saist thou) you are
a merry man M. *Dicke*, it befits not the wise to mocke
a man in miserie. In truth thou saist true *Tom* , and for
my mindes sake I would not for a shilling but that thou
hadst beene in prison, it hath made my worship so me-
ry: but because thou continuest my precepts that am a
Cambridge-man, from whence all vertue flowes , and
is the very fountaine and Cunduit-head of all learning.
O heere I could praise Cambridge an houre by the
clocke.

Therefore I say, for thy contempt of me I will call thy
keeper, and tell how th'art stolne out of prison & come
to mee to helpe thee off with thy shackles. Noe *Thomas*
noe, I am no pick-locke, I thanke God. I liue without
picking, though thou liuest not without lockes. But
are you gone, thou wert afraid of thy keeper, goe to the
place from whence you came, &c. with a knaues name

to

to you. b: Ha, ha, if I had but followed this matter euen
a little more, I could haue perswaded thee to liue and
dye in prison.

Alas, I could doo anie thing with thee now, all thy
senses are so taken downe Happie (quoth I) in prison?
haplesse indeed, How happie is the owle caught fast in
a lyme-bough, when all the smaller birdes doo chatter
at her for ioye ? How happie the Rat caught in a trappe,
and there dies a liuing death ? How happie the tyred
hart striken of the Hunter, who runnes panting, consu-
ming her breath, and at last faints for want of breath?
how happie the wearied hare pursued with dogs, euer
looking when they shall teare her in peeces ? and how
happie the cunny-catching weasell insnared in the Par-
kers net, and hangd vpon a tree ? thus happie art thou:
with the owle thou art lymed and wondred at, with the
Rat thou art sore prest, with the Hart thou art in a con-
sumption, with the hare thou alwaies expectest a teare-
ing, and with the weasell thou shalt be hanged. All these
torments are in prison, a demi hell, where (like fiends)
the prisoners crawle about in chaines, euerie one per-
plext with his seuerall paine ; a darksome laborynth, out
of which thou canst neuer passe, though guided by a
thred.

O double vnhappie soule of thine, thrie diues so
doubly imprisoned, first in thy bodie, which is a more
stinking prison than this where thou art ; then, that it ac-
companieth thy bodie in this prison. Were it not sufficient that one prison should tortor thy soule enough?
No, first because thy soule hath too deepe a hand in all
thy knaueries, tis so imprisoned and fettered to thy bodie, that it cannot go without it Poore Sonke, more miserable than the kings daughter captiuated & long time
kept imprisoned in the Theeues houses, at last offering

*Apostro-
phe.
Apuleius*

10

to breake away, was condemned to be sewed into the
asses bodie, & there to dye; for the asses bodie was dead,
and nothing aliue in the asse (the prison) to trouble the
Maid the prisoner. But thy prison is aliue, and all the af-
fections in thy bodie are as stinking vermine & wormes
in it, that crawle about thee, gnawing thee, and putting
thee to miserie. She in short time was sure to die, and so
to be free againe; thou art still in dying, and hoping for
freedome, but still liuest, and this augments thy calamitie : she should haue had her head left out to breathe into the aire, but thou breathest into thy prison thy bodie,
that corrupts within thee, and so retournes to bee thyne
owne poyson. Thus much miserie (poore soule) thine
owne bodie affoords thee, and by being with thy bodie
in the second prison, all this is doubled. Now if thou
wouldest bee free from thy prisons, make a hoale in thy
Continua- first prison, breake out there, and so thou escapest both,
ta Meta- thou neuer canst be caught again : and by this thou shalt
phora. crie quittance with thy bodie, that thus hath tormented
thee, and shalt leaue him buried in a perpetuall dungeon.

Here let mee giue a cut or two on thy latest bred excrements, before I goe to the finishing of the perfect
Cut.

A littie lumpe of lead, while it is round will lye in a
small roome, but being beaten it will spread broad, and
require a larger place to containe it ; and a roape bound
fast vp, might easily be couered, but vnfolded & drawne
out at length, it hardly can bee hidden ; so you (simply
considered) are of no report, but if you bee vntrust and
beaten out, & your actions all vnfolded, your name cannot be limitted. And now you, hauing a care of your
credite, scorning to lie wrapt vp in obliuion the moth of
fame, haue augmented the stretche-out line of your
deedes, by that most infamous, most dunsicall and thrice
oppro-

opprobrious worke *The Ile of Dogs :* for which you are
greatly in requeſt; that, as when a ſtone is caſt into the
water, manie circles ariſe from it, and one ſucceedeth a-
nother, that if one goeth not round, the other following might be adioyned to it, and ſo make the full circle :
ſo, if ſuch infinite ſtore of your deedes are not ſufficient
to purchaſe to you eternall ſhame and ſorrow, there ariſe
from you more vnder then to helpe forward : and laſt of
all commeth this your laſt worke, which maketh all ſure,
and leaueth a ſigne behinde it.   And of this your laſt *Cropt ears*
worke, I muſt needes ſay ſomewhat : for ſeeing that this
my firſt work & off-ſpring hath remained in my womb
beyond the time allotted, it muſt needs be growen greater ; and if it become a monſter, it muſt needes be in ex-
ceſſe.

O yes, O yes : if there bee anie manner of *A procla-*
man, perſon or perſons, can bring anye ti- *mation for*
dings of Tho : Nashe Gentleman, let hym *T. Nashe.*
come and giue knovvledge thereof, & hee
shalbe plenteouſly revvarded.

Hearke you *Thomas,* the Crier calls you. What, a
fugitiue ? how comes that to paſſe, that thou a man of ſo
good an education, & ſo wel backt by the Muſes, ſhuldſt
prooue a fugitiue ? But alas, thy Muſes brought thee to
this miſerie : you and your Muſes maye euen goe hang
your ſelues : now you may wiſh, that he that firſt put the
Muſes into your head, had knockt out your hornes. But
ſeeing it hath ſo happened, call for your *Thalia* among
your Muſes, let her play ſome muſique, and I will dar ce

F

at your hanging? But twas prouidence in thee, to fore-see thy woe, and to labour to eschew it, if not by auer-ring what you haue said, and standing too it, yet by she-wing your heeles. For as is the Prouerbe ; *Vbi leonina pellis insufficiens est, vulpina astutia assuenda est.* If by strong hand you cannot obtaine it, light heeles are to be required : for one paire of legs are worth two payre of hands. And of all the parts of thy bodie, thy legges are thy most trustie seruants : for in all thy life when as thou couldest not obtaine of anie of the parts of thy bodie to effect thy will, yet legs thou hadst to commaund for to walke and flee whethersoeuer was thy pleasure, neither now in this extremitie doo they deceiue thee. O, how much art thou beholding to thy legs? *Bankes* was not so much beholding to his Horse, that serued to ride on, and to doo such wonderfull crankes, as thou art to thy leggs, which haue thus cunningly conuayed thee. If euerie begger by the high wayes side (hauing his legs corrupt-ed and halfe destroyed with botches, byles and fistulaes) maketh much of them, getteth stilts and creepeth easily on them, for feare of hurting them, because they main-taine them, and prooue better vnto them than manie an honest Trade; then why shouldest not thou (by an argument *a malo in peius*)make much of thy legs, which by speedie carriage of thee from place to place to get the victualls, doo not onely maintaine thy life, but also at this time haue saued thy life, by their true seruice vnto thee. Wherefore (these things considered) thou canst not chuse but in all humilitie offer thy old shooes for sa-crifice to *Thetis* for thy swift feet. And twas wisely done of that high dread Liech *Apollo* to appoint *Pisces* the Signe to the feete, to shew that a man should be as swift as a fish about his affaires. Nerethelesse can I accuse you of lazines, : for all this time of your vagation, with you

I

I thinke the Signe hath been in *Pisces.* Now in this thy flight thou art a night-bird, for the day wil bewray thee: the Bat and the Owle be thy fellow trauellers. But to come roundly vnto you, this cannot long continue: the Owle sometime is snarld in the day season, and olde Father Time at length will bring you to light. Therefore, were you as well prouided to continue your flight, as is the beast *Ephemeron*, which because shee hath but one day to liue, hath manie legs, foure wings, and all what Nature can affoord, to giue her expedition to see about the world for her one dayes pleasure: or as *Pegasus* that winged Horse, which in swiftnes equalleth the Horses of the Sunne, which in one naturall day perambulate all the world: or as the beast *Alce*, which runneth on the snow with such celeritie that shee neuer sinketh vnto the ground: Were you (I say) as swift as anie of these, you shall be catcht, such is your destinie: and then your punishment shall be doubled on you, both for your flying, and your other villanie

Since that thy Ile of Dogs hath made thee thus miserable, I cannot but account thee a Dog, and chyde and rate thee as a Dog that hath done a fault. And yet doo not I know why I should blame Dogs? for *Can*, which signifieth a Dog, is also a most trustie Seruant; for that Dogs are faithfull Seruants, to whome their Masters in the night time giue in charge all their treasure. They are at commaund to waite vpon their Masters, whether they bend their iourney, to fight for them against their Enemies, and to spend their liues to defend them, and to offend their aduersaries, as we read of King *Cazament*: who beeing exilde, brought with him from banishment two hundreth Dogges, which (with wonderfull fiercenesse) warred against their resistants: in whom hee reposed much more confidence & hope of victorie, again

F 2

to

to be seated in his throne, than if hee had been defended by a mightie hoast of armed men.   And *Iasors* dogge, his master being dead, neuer would eate anie meate, but with great griefe and hunger died for companie.   *Tycius* the *Sabine* had a dogge which accompanied hym to prison, and when he was dead, he remained howling by the carcasse: to whom when one cast meate, he laid it to the mouth of his dead master, to reuiue him againe: and when his corpes was throwen into the riuer *Tybris*, the dogge leapt after it, so that all the people wondered at the loue of this faithfull creature. *Pyrrhus* the King going a iourney, came by a dogge which kept the bodie of a dead man : which when hee saw, he comaunded the bodie to be buried, and the dogge to bee brought home with him : this done, a few dayes after came souldiours before the King, among whom the dogge espyed them which killd his master, and barked incessantly at them ; sometime looking and fawning on the King, and then barked againe. At which signe the King astonished, examined them, and vpon light examinations they confessed the murder, and tooke punishment for it.   Further, we read of a dogge called *Capparus* in *Athens*, which in the night pursude a theefe that robbed a Church, & being driuen backe with stones by the Theefe, followed him aloofe off, but alwayes kept him in sight, and at last came to him, and sat by him while he slept.   The next morne, so soone as euer the Sunnes golden crowne gan to appeare, and his fierie steedes trapperd in their capparisons set on their wonted race, the theefe fleeing, the dogge stil kept his chase, and complaind in his language to the passengers of the theefe. At last he was taken and brought backe, before whom the dog came all the way leaping and exulting for ioy, as to whome all the prayse was due for this deed.

The

The *Athenians* decreed that for this publique good, the dogge fhould be kept by publique charges, and the care of his keeping was alwaies afterward layd vpon the Priefts. And I feare mee, and almoft diuine fo much, that the verie dogges (wherefoeuer thou plaift leaft in fight) will bewraye thee and bring thee to thy torture. Againe, (among the *Aegiptians*) *Saturne* was called *Kyon*, becaufe as a pregnant woman, he begat all things of himfelfe and in himfelfe ; and in antique time they worfhipped dogges, and had them in great account till on a time when *Cambyfes* killed a man and caft hym away, no other beaft but a dog rauened in the dead carcaffe.

Laftly, to come neerer to your felfe, you fhall heare of a dogge that was an excellent Actor. In *Rome* there was a Stage-player, which fet out a Hiftorie of diuers perfonages, among whom there was a dogge to be poifoned and reuiue againe ; a Part of no leffe difficultie than the king or the clowne, and was as well perfourmed : for (at his time) he eate the poyfon, and prefently (drunkard-like) ftackered vp and downe, reeling backward and forward, bending his head to the ground, as if it were too heauie for his bodie, as his Part was ; and at laft fell downe, ftretcht himfelfe vpon the ftage, and lay for dead. Soone after, when his Cue was fpoken, firft by little and little he began to mooue himfelfe, and then ftretching forth his legs as though he awaked from a deepe fleepe, and lifting vp his head, lookt about him: then he arofe, and came to him to whom his part was he fhould come : which thing (befides the great pleafure) mooued wonderfull admiration in olde *Vefpafian* the Emperour there prefent, and in all the other that were fpectators.

Thefe prettie tales of dogges might keepe mee from

chi-

chiding of thee, but thou art no such dogge; thefe were all well nurtured when they were whelps, you not fo, the worme was not pluckt out from vnder your tongue, fo that you haue run mad, and bit venome euer fince: for thefe are the properties of a mad dog.

Firft, the blacke choller which raigneth in them turneth to madnes moft commonly in the Spring-time and in Autumne: and you though you are mad all the yeere, yet haue fhewed the figne of it efpecially this laft Autumne; they alwaies run with their mouthes open and their tongues hanging out, wee know howe wide your mouth is, how long your tung; your mouth is neuer fhut, your tongue neuer tyed : flauer and fome fall from their iawes as they run, and tis but flauer that proceedeth from thy mouth: though their eyes be open, yet they ftumble on euery obiect; fo though thou feeft who offends thee not, yet thou all offendeft: they whofoeuer are bitten with a mad dog alfo run mad, and they whom thy vlcered tongue did bite, are fo ftirred vp by it, that till they haue got you and wormed you, they cannot be well : thus you may fee to what mifery you were borne. Woe to the teats of thy Dam that gaue thee fuck, and woe to blind fortune, that fhe opened not her eyes to fee to affoord thee better fortune : and woe to the dog-daies, for in thofe thou wroughteft that which now works thy woe, take heede heerafter what you doe in dog-daies. The natures fecretaries record of that kinde of goate cald *Oryx*, that all the yeere her throate is fhut, the ftrings of her voice tyed, til dog-daies come, & then that very day and houre in which the dog-ftarre firft appeareth (at which time dog-daies begin) fhee openeth her voyce and crieth : the like miracle thefe laft dog-daies haue done of thee, for what all the whole yeere could not bring to paffe, and all the Country long haue

ex-

expected, that is, thy confusion, these dog-dayes by thine owne wordes haue effected: therfore happy hadst thou beene if thou hadst remained still in London, that thou mightest haue beene knockt on the with many of thy fellowes these dog-daies, for nowe the further thou fleest, the further thou runst into thy calamitie: there is watch layd for you, you cannot escape; th'art in as ill a taking as the Hare, which being all the day hunted, at last concludes to dye, for (said she) whether should I flye to escape these dogs, if I should flye to heauen, there is *canis sidus celeste*: if I should run into the sea, there is *ca-* *The dogs* *nis piscis marinus*, and heere on earth millions of dogges *starre.* seeke to torment me; aye me, heauen, earth and sea con- *The dogs* spire my tragedy: and as wofull as the Cunny which e- *fish.* scaping the Weasell fell into the hunters net, of which was that pythie Epigram, Would to God the Weasell with my bloud had sucked out my life, for nowe I am kept a pray for the rauening dogs, and cruell-harted mã sits laughing whilst my body is broken vp, and my guts deuided into many shares: and though yet thou hast e- scaped thy snares, it will not bee long ere thou beest ta- ken and then the'rs laughing worke for all the Country; for though thy body were shared into infinite indiui- duals, yet euery one could not haue his part whome thou hast abused, for recompence for thy iniury done vnto him.

Nowe let mee see thy punishment for thy Isle of dogges, tis an auncient custome in our Countrie when wee take a dogge that hath done a fault, presently to crop his eares, and this surely for thy fault is thy pu- nishment, but why (might some say) are thine eares pu- nished for thy tongues fault?

I

I answere, thine eares are worthy to be punished for not discharging their office, for whereas they should heare before thou speakest, as they that be skilfull at the ball, first receiue the ball before they cast it foorth a-gaine; and into a vessel there is first infusion before there be effusion out of the same; the ouer pregnant dog (we see) bringeth forth blinde puppies, and the spider that prepares her matter and weaues her webbe together at the same time, makes but slender worke of it, and easie to be broken of euery flye. I say, whereas thou shouldst first haue heard, thou first speakest, thy tongue was in thy eares place, and for this cause thine eares are iustly punished.

Nature gaue thee two eares and but one tongue be-cause thou shouldst heare more then thou shouldest speake but because thou hast spoke more than euer thou heardst, thine eares shall bee taken from thee : She set thine eyes and thine eares both of equall highnes and alwaies open, that they might bee ready to heare and to see, but thy tongue she put into a case that it might bee slowe to speake; but thine eares were dull to heare, and thy tongue too quicke of speach: Therefore thine eares deserue their punishment : Then to bee short, to haue *Ha ha ha.* thine cropt is thy punishment : What *Tom*, are thine eares gone? *O fine man will you buy a fine dog?* Why thou *Crop-eard* art in the fashion, thou art priuiledged to weare long *first wore* lockes by ancient charter, but now if the fashion were *lockes.* as hot as euer twas to weare ringes in their eares, faith thou must weare thine euen in thy tongue, because that cosoned thee of thine eares: are thy eares so moueable? art thou a monster? indeede all beasts haue free mouing of their eares graunted to them, but for men I neuer knew any but thee haue their eares mouing, and thine I see to haue the gentle quite remoue : I thinke tis a dis-

cafe,

eafed, for I am affure tis a horible paine to bee troubled
with the mouing of the eares. I coniecture no goodnes
by this ftrange accident of moueable eares this yere , I
hope fhortly we fhall haue Ballads out of it. I am afraid
I tell you by this ftrange figne that we fhall haue a wet
winter this yere, for if it be true(which the Philofophers
affirme) that when an Affes eares hang downe toward
the ground,tis a certaine figne of raine inftant, then feeing thine eares not only hang toward the ground , but
euen drop down to the ground, how can it chufe but be
a figne of great wet at hand? and to thee it fhould be a
caufe of perpetuall fhowers that fhould flow from thine
eyes, but thou art diye, no droppe of grace from thine
eyes. If taking away of thine eares could take away thy
hearing too , twere fome profit for thee, for then thou
fhouldft not heare thy felfe raild on , laughed at , nor
know thy felfe to be a mocking ftocke to all the Country but there is a more plaine way made to thy hearing
organs , fo that thou fhalt more lightly heare thy felfe
euery where cald crop-eard curre. What wilt thou giue
me if I (I am a Chirurgion)make a new paire of eares
grow out of thy head, which paffeth *Appolloes* cunning,
that fo thou maift ftil liue with fame in thine own countrie, or if I heale them as though thou neuer hadft any ,
that I may goe with thee into Germanie and there fhew
thee for a ftrange beaft bred in England , with a face like
a man, with no eares, with a tung like a venomous Serpent, and a nofe like no body. The laft I care not if I con-
fented to: if thou woldft liue in good order but one half
yere, but to the firft that is to giue thee new eares, I neuer
wil grant thogh thou fholdft be infpired to liue orderly
al the refidue of thy life, no though I had wax & al things
ready, for long agoe haft thou deferued this difgrace to
be earelefle, euer fince thou beganft to write , for libels
deferue that punifhment, and euery booke which yet

G   thou

thou haſt written is a libell, and whomſoeuer thou na-
meſt in thy booke hath a libell made of him, thou pur-
poſing to ſpeake well of him; ſuch is the malice of thy
cankerd tongue. Therefore thou deſeruedſt to looſe
thine eares for naming the Biſhop of *Ely* and of *Lin-
colne*, and for writing of *Chriſtes teares ouer Ieruſalem*:
how dareſt thou take ſuch holy matters into thy ſtinking mouth, ſo to defile and polute them? your Dildoe &
ſuch ſubiects are fit matter for you, for of thoſe you cannot ſpeak amiſſe, the more you raile of the the neerer you
touch the matter : but becauſe you were not puniſhed
for thoſe libels, you began your olde courſe againe, *canis ad vomitum*, you began to chew the cud of your villanie and to bring more libels into light. But I hope this
laſt libell will reuenge the reſt.

We heare howe you threatned to ſpoile our ſtirring
Satiriſt: alas, haue thy writings ſuch efficacie? indeed they
are poyſoned, but poiſon will not worke on euery ſubiect: and if thou ſhouldſt but name him, ſo that it might
giue but any blemiſh to his fame, aſſure thy ſelfe to bee
met withal of troops of Scholers which wil ſoone make
thee be one of *Terence* his paraſits: in wounds thou ſhalt
exceed *Caſſianus* which was ſo pittifully pinked of his
own Schollers: & now whilſt I am in the hot inuectiue I
haue a meſſage to doe to you, the townſmen of *Cherri-
hinton* ſend you comendations, & they demaund a reſon
of you why you call them clownes? they ſay, they neuer
offered you any wrong, wherefore if euer you come that
way, they will ſend all the dogs in the town after you to
pluck off your ears if they be not gone before you come.
Now I thinke it be time to remember my promiſe to the
readers, that is that I be not irkeſome to them with
tediouſnes, that ſo they might with good acceptance
digeſt what hetherto they haue read: therefore I will
drawe toward an end and ſo finiſh this perfect Cut.

Where

Wheras thou commendst thy Epistle to me as a garment for a foole, and therefore that it should bee long: I (as is thy desire) haue cut it with my scissers, layd it ope, and according to that pattern haue made a coate for thy selfe, but it is so short that thou shalt not neede to curtaile it, for some fooles haue long coates for that cause onely, that they might the better hide their folly and cover their nakednes, which els all should see, yet I haue made thy coate short and little, that by thy behauiour in it thou mayst bewray to others thy simplicitie, & if I had tooke in hand to haue made it great enough to couer al thy folly, this is not the twentith part of stuffe that wold haue serued, neither possibly couldst thou haue had thy new coate against this time: but seeing thy garment is dispatcht for thee, weare it and vse it well, for the fashion of long cloathes is wearing away, & short cloaths will shortly be in request againe, and then thou shalt be a foole of the fashion, as soone as the proudest of them all.

Againe, this coate for thy body and the coole irons for thy legges will be a most cooling sute for thee all this Summer time, therefore make much of it, let it not bee thy euery day sute, but as the *Utopians* were wont to make them sutes of leather, which lasted seuen yeeres, in which they did all their labour, and when they went abroad they cast on their cloakes which hid their leather cloathes and made them seeme comely and handsome: so if thou canst but get some old, greasie, cast fustian sute to weare within dores, this coate will serue thee to cast on to iet abroad in, and doe thee credit.

Wherefore (good *Tom*) I exhort thee to keepe thee (whilst thou art) in good case, thou art well apparelled, it may bee thou presently wilt bestowe a coate of mee, doe not so, all thy coates are threed-

bare

bare and I neede them not, though thou hast many, for
I know thou hast three or foure coates ready made (like
a saleman) for some body: then, to which soeuer thou
sowest but a patch or two concerning me, that coat shal
serue me: thou puttest diuers stuffe into one coate, and
this is thy vse in all thy confutations, as in this thy book
thou bringest into the partie against whom thou writest,
his brothers, which argueth (as I sayd before) want of
inuention, but it skils not, thou art priuiledged neuer to
goe from the matter, it might as well bee permitted in
thee as in the historian that promising to speake of the
faith of the Iewes, made a long tale of *Nilus* : but (as I
said) be a good husband *Tom* and keep thy coate to thy
selfe, thou wilt need them al, and when this coate which
which I bestowe on thee shall waxe threed-bare, I will
dresse it for thee the second time and giue it thee a-
gaine.

This I speak not to wage discord against thee, but rather to make an end of all iarres, that as wife & husband
will brawle and be at mortall sewde al the day long, but
when boord or bed time come they are friendes againe
and louingly kisse one an other : so though hetherto we
haue disagreed and beene at oddes, yet this one coate
shall containe vs both, which thou shalt weare as the
cognisaunce of my singuler loue towards thee, that wee
liuing in mutuall loue may so dye, and at last louing like
two brothers *Castor* and *Pollux*, or the two sisters *Vrsa
maior* and *Vrsa minor* wee may bee carried vp to heauen
together, and there translated into two starres.

Finally these thinges considered aright, in loue
I beseech thee (that thou maist see I am not past
grace) to suffer mee to retort thy grace, and so to end,
which my selfe will follow for you; you suing *sub forma
pauperis.*

A

A Grace in the behalfe of Thomas Nashe.

To all ballet-makers, pamphleters, preſſe hanters, boon pot poets, and ſuch like, to whom theſe preſents ſhall come, greeting, Wheras *Tho: Naſhe* the bearer heereof, borne I know not where, educated ſometime at *Cambridge :* where (being diſtracted of his wits) he fell into diuers miſdemeanors, which were the firſt ſteps that broght him to this poore eſtate. As namely in his freſh-time how he floriſhed in all impudencie toward Schollers, and abuſe to the Townſmen; inſomuch, that to this daye the Towneſ-men call euerie vntoward Scholler of whome there is great hope, *a verie Naſhe.* Then being Bachelor of Arte, which by great labour he got, to ſhew afterward that he was not vnworthie of it, had a hand in a Show called *Terminus & non terminus,* for which his partener in it was expelled the Colledge : but this foreſaid *Naſhe* played in it (as I ſuppoſe) the Varlet of Clubs; which he acted with ſuch naturall affection, that all the ſpectators tooke him to be the verie ſame. Then ſuſpecting himſelfe that he ſhould be ſtaied for *egregie dunſus,* and not attain to the next Degree, ſaid he had commenſt enough, and ſo forſooke *Cambridge,* being Batchelor of the third yere. Then he raiſd himſelfe vnto an higher Clime, no leſſe than *London* could ſerue him : where ſomewhat reeouered of his wits, by the excrements thereof (for the ſpace of nine or ten yere) hee hath got his belly fed and his backe cloathed. As alſo I hope you are not ignoraunt how hee hath troubled the Preſſe all this time, and publiſhed ſundrie workes & volumes, which I take with me as humble fellow-ſuters to you, that you being all in one ſtraine (and that very low, he in a higher key) you would vouchſafe to take him as your graduate Captain generall in all villanie : to which villanie conioyn your voyces and in which villanie praye

and

and say together, *Viuat, moriatur Nashe.* To these pre-misses, that they are true, and that hee among you all is onely worthie this title, I (as head Lecturer) put too my hand.

Richard Lichfield.

But *Tom*, thy selfe art past grace : for some of thyne owne faction, enuying thy proficiencie and honour to which thou aspirest, hath pocketted thy Grace. O en-uie, catterpiller to vertue !   But let him know that thou hast a Patron will sticke to thee, and that thou art graci-ous in more Faculties than one, I will put vp another Grace for thee, wherein he shall haue no voyce, and one onely man an old frend of thine shall strike it dead.

A Grace in the behalfe of Thomas Nashe, to the right worshipfull and grand Commander of all the superrants & subtercubants of Englands great Metropolis, the Prouost Marshall of London.

FOrasmuch as *Thomas Nash* sundrie and oftentimes hath been cast into manie prisons (by full authori-tie) for his mis-behauiors, and hath polluted them all, so that there is not one prison in *London*, that is not infected with *Nashes euill :* and being lately set at libertie, rangeth vp and downe, gathering poyson in e-uerie place, whereby he infecteth the common aire ; I am to desire you, that as you tender the common good of the weale publike, and as the vertue of your office re-quireth which is to clense the City of all vitious and vn-ruly persons, when this aboue named *Nashe* shall hap-pen into your presinctes or dioces of your authority you would giue him his vnction in the highest degree, and clense vs quite of him, which you shall effect thus. Send
him

him not to prisons any more which are corrupted by
him already, but commit him to the *Proctter of the Spittle*,
where hee shall not stay long least hee breed a plague a-
mong them also: but passe frō him to Bull, who by your
permission hauing ful power ouer him and being of such
amiable and dexterious facility in discharging his duety,
will soone knit the knot of life and death vpon him, strō-
ger then that Gordian knot neuer to bee loosed, and by
that pritty tricke of fast and loose, will loose your Cittie
from him and him from all his infections, and will hang
him in so sweet & cleer a prospect as that it wilbe greatly to your credit to see the great concourse thether of all
sects of people: as first, I with my brethren the Barber-
Chirurgions of London, wil be there, because we cannot
phlebotamize him, to anatomize him and keep his bons
as a chronicle to shew many ages heereafter that sometime liued such a man, our posteritie hauing by traditi-
on what he was, and you in some part might be chroni-
cled (as well as S.George) for destroying this serpent: thē
there will flock all the Cunni-catchers of London to see
the portraiture of the arch architectour of their arte: lastly, al the Ballad-makers of London his very enimies that
stayed his last grace, will be there to heare his confession,
and out of his last words will make Epitaphes of him, &
afterward Ballads of the life and death of *Thomas Nash*.
Let this grace passe as soone as may bee, if not for any
perticular loue to him, yet as you are a Magistrate of the
Cittie, and ought to knowe what tis to prefer a publike
commodititie: if this grace passe not, hee is like to bee
stayde finally till the next yeere. I his head-lecturer present him to you.

Richard Lichfield.

This

Thus (curteous Gentlemen) I haue brought you to the ende of his trimming, though he be not so curiously done as he deserueth : hold mee excused, hee is the first man that euer I cut on this fashion. And if perhaps in this Trimming I haue cut more partes of him than are necessarie, let mee heare your censures, and in my next Cut I will not be so lauish : but as the Curate, who when he was first instald into his Benefice, and among other Iniunctions being inioynd (as the order is) to forewarne his Parish of Holy-daies, that they might fast for them: and thinking all those Holy daies which hee saw in hys Calender written with red letters, on a time said to hys Parishioners, You must fast next wensday for Saint *Sol in Virgo,* which is on thursday, because he saw it in red letters. Which mooued laughter to the wife of the Pa-rish; who presently instructed him, that ouer what red words soeuer he saw *Fast* written, those hee should bid Holi-dayes : so in short time he became expert in it. In like manner, I hauing but newly taken Orders in these affaires, if heere I haue been too prodigall in *snip snaps,* tell me of it, limit me with a Fast, and in short time you shall see me reformed.

FINIS.

The following blank pages in this copy have been inserted to allow for a better binding.